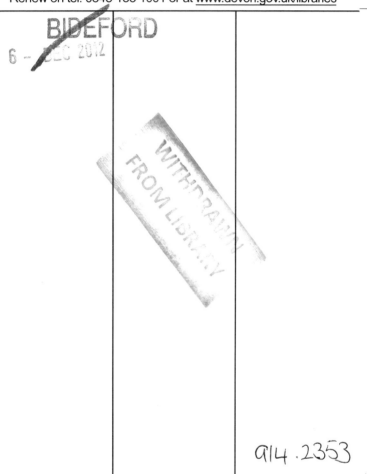

DARTMOOR
A Winter's Tale

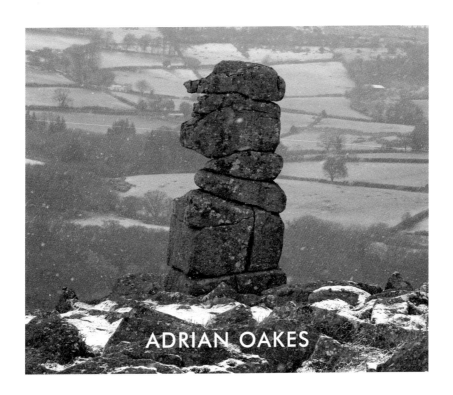

ADRIAN OAKES

HALSGROVE

First published in Great Britain in 2009

British Library Cataloguing-in-Publication Data
A CIP record for this title is available from the British Library

ISBN 978 1 84114 866 3

HALSGROVE
Halsgrove House,
Ryelands Industrial Estate,
Bagley Road, Wellington, Somerset TA21 9PZ
Tel: 01823 653777   Fax: 01823 216796
email: sales@halsgrove.com

Part of the Halsgrove group of companies
Information on all Halsgrove titles is available at: www.halsgrove.com

Printed and bound in India on behalf of JFDi Print Services Ltd

Introduction

I have walked Dartmoor for over twenty years, drawn back to it after visits as a child, and more recently I have climbed, clambered and waited patiently to gain the best opportunity for the camera. Through forest, past stone rows and into ancient medieval settlements I am never short of inspiration.

Walking the moor in winter can be hugely rewarding, and in my opinion the season offers the best light and colours of the year. The landscape is usually clear, without the haze often present in summer.

Early on a cold and sunny November day, walking the open moor around Scorhill circle, I looked across towards Watern Tor, surrounded in total silence, thinking to myself 'How can so many people live so close and not experience this?'

Early 2009 brought heavy snow. Accessing the moor was a great challenge but I managed to capture some of the amazing scenes the weather created. My thoughts were with the people who lived and worked on the moor, now and in winters' past, and the hardships they endured.

I intend to continue visiting and photographing Dartmoor for many years as it possesses a magnetism that will always draw me back. My aim, when selecting the images for this book, was to capture the essence of winter on Dartmoor, its superb landscapes and unique atmosphere.

Adrian Oakes 2009
www.adrianoakes.com

A steep climb rewarded me with a superb clear view over the winter gorse to Burrator reservoir, with Sheepstor rising in the background.

Above:
A cold winter day at Ger Tor above Tavy Cleave.

Right:
From Honeybag Tor this sunrise initially started grey and overcast.
Then, with amazing luck, the sun broke through and illuminated Haytor on the horizon.

Above:
Midwinter, while travelling across the Moor, I passed this farm entrance buried in deep snow. But someone had ventured out after the heavy snowfall.

Right:
Dartmoor has many Logan Stones such as this one silhouetted at sunset.
These have been described somewhat ponderously, as 'rocks that have become disjoined from the parent rock and can be rocked without fear of falling'.

Above:
A lone Dartmoor pony grazes in the frost near Princetown, obviously
not worried about the light coating of snow on its back.

Left:
A lone ram wanders on the open moor at sunset.

The Longstone on Chagford Common on a bitter winter morning. The sun tries in vain to break through the mist.

Wonderful quality of light can be enjoyed in winter, as with this view over Haytor vale.

A skeletal but apparently healthy tree stands waiting for spring. A cut granite block lies nearby, hewn from the nearby quarry.

A lone skier takes full advantage of the conditions on the slopes below Haytor.

A striking and colourful sky above Rippon Tor.

This old granite thatched cottage, once an inn, overlooks Hound Tor.

Whilst on a walk on a fine winter's morning, I was greeted by this inquisitive and soaked Dartmoor pony.

View from the top of Great Tor rocks that lie between Hound Tor (seen in the distance) and Haytor.

Many tiny waterfalls can be found on the moor, such as this one, surrounded by colourful winter foliage near Buckland.

A twisted and beaten tree refuses to give into the elements.

I came across this well-preserved cast-iron signpost near Peter Tavy.

A snowy landscape on a very cold, but bright, winter's morning.

Left:
One of Dartmoor's ancient clapper bridges. This one stands at Scorhill, near Batworthy, bridging the North Teign.

A walker and his dog enjoy a walk on a January morning at Buckland Beacon.

Widecombe-in-the-Moor. The village sits within the valley of the East Webburn river and is famous for its September Fair, and the characters, including Uncle Tom Cobley, that appear in the song 'Widecombe Fair'.

Looking towards Saddle Tor, with leafless trees standing out against the white landscape.

A weather-beaten tree leans over a drystone wall near the Warren House Inn.
I find rowan and hawthorn trees provide more interesting images when devoid of foliage.

One brisk climb rewarded me with a fantastic view from the top of Hookney Tor towards Widecombe-in-the-Moor. Nearby is the Bronze Age settlement of Grimspound.

Bennetts Cross decorated with a Christmas wreath. This is one of Dartmoor's best known and most accessible stone crosses and is thought to be at least 300 years old.

Above:
The snow covered Pepperpot in Chagford
market square.

Left:
Pathway to Chagford church in heavy snow.

Panorama from Howell Tor looking towards Haytor.

The tiny church of St Michael De Rupe on the rock outcrop at Brentor.

Right:
A cut granite block at sunset, with Foggintor Quarry in the distance. The now-disused quarry provided granite for the construction of Nelson's Column in Trafalgar Square.

Gorse covered in ice and snow.

The granite outcrop of Bowerman's Nose in midwinter. The sky seems to part either side of this distinctive landmark. Legend has it that this is the hunter Bowerman, turned to stone by witches, while the numerous stones littered around the base are the hounds.

Dartmoor is well known for its treacherous peat bogs, mainly found on the higher moor. They may look harmless and passable but they are not to be underestimated. I once tried the well known art of 'bog hopping' between grass clumps near the West Okement valley and slipped in up to my knees!

Dartmoor pony.

33

Above:
HM Prison, Princetown in the snow. It first was built to house Napoleonic prisoners of war in 1806.

Right:
Drift patterns in the snow picked out by the early winter light

Above:
Bitter winds at sunrise blow snow over the road. It is worth enduring such temperatures
in order to capture scenes such as this.

Right:
Early morning light and long shadows at Saddletor. Haytor sits in the sun on the horizon.

An ancient wooded farm track near Hucken Tor bathed in winter light.

Opposite:
The best known clapper bridge on Dartmoor, at Postbridge. I stood in the river to capture this image, with the tiny fall and the surrounding snow. Little did I know until it was too late that my wellingtons were filling with ice-cold water.

My favourite waterfall along the lower end of Tavy Cleave. The pool below it is called the 'Devils Kitchen'.

Freshly cut logs near Yellowmead Farm on the ancient granite railway track to Foggintor.

Right:
I have passed this tree many times over the years and thought 'one day I will capture that gateway in the snow'. I was lucky to take the picture with the sun breaking through the branches of the tree.

Gateway to Rippon Tor on a day with a cool clear blue sky.

Left:
A fantastic morning sky casts a shadow behind Rippon Tor and illuminates the landscape. To have snow and the sun together is truly wonderful.

A glorious billowing winter sky breaks over Peek Hill looking from Sharpitor.

Granite posts stand alongside Manaton Green, with St Winifreds Church in the background.

One of my favourite locations is the Staple Tors group. This sunset was taken over the distinctive shapes of Great Staple Tor. The light that evening was fantastic. Quite a walk to the car in the dark though...

Right:
Sheep graze in the winter sun near Princetown. Dartmoor would not be the same without the livestock that seem to wander freely. I always stay within the speed limit and keep my eyes peeled as sheep and cattle roam alongside and across the roads.

Left:
A clear view of Great Mis Tor from Pew Tor rocks.

DRIVE WITH MOOR CARE

Bowerman's Nose on a dark grey day as snow showers move in.

Left:
A view over a granite drystone wall towards Haytor Vale.

Panorama looking from Sharpitor to Peek Hill beneath a dramatic sky.

The Horseshoe Falls, named due to their shape, are a short walk from New Bridge. The late afternoon light, that one only really sees in winter, creates wonderful soft colours in the water and also allows a long shutter speed to soften the water.

A rider enjoys the winter morning light on Chagford Common. I have been fortunate to ride across the moor, a fantastic experience. I had to be quick with this shot as the rider said the horse was keen to gallop.

Haytor silhouette at sunrise. A bitter wind howled around the rocks blowing a fine mist of snow and ice.

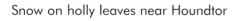

Snow on holly leaves near Houndtor

Late evening light on the rocks looking towards the Grimspound Bronze Age settlement.

A wonderful and regularly photographed lone tree at Howell Tor. I ran across the Moor to get to this shot before the light faded. I just had time to capture the sun star through the branches.

A hut circle at Grimspound. This ancient Bronze Age settlement comprises a giant ring of stones that would have formed a perimeter wall. Within can be found the remains of huts and livestock pens. Hookney Tor sits in the distance.

Ice-covered rocks on a Dartmoor river in midwinter.

Icicles on the falls at Tavy Cleave. Tavy Cleave rises in the background.
The Cleave is unusual as it runs through a river valley enclosed by a steep gorge.

Ice crystals and moss.

Icy rapids in the Tavy Cleave valley.

January 2009 saw temperatures as low as –12 degrees Celsius.
Giant icicles hung from virtually every rock along this river.

In the 1800s Pew Tor was the victim of 'Graniteers' who quarried much of the stone.

January skies billow over the Cave-Penney Memorial cross near Corndon Tor. This sits 1300 ft above sea level and is a memorial to a brave soldier who died in the First World War. At the bottom of the inscription it reads 'Look up and lift your heads' and considering the view from here it is very apt.

I climbed Kes Tor before sunrise to be rewarded with the sun just breaking the horizon and pools of water gently illuminated in hollows on the top of the Tor. The Tor can be found near Batworthy on the edge of Chagford Common.

Hookney Tor in the late afternoon.

A brief walk in the pine woods near Burrator and I am greeted by the sun breaking through the trees and lighting up the ground around me.

Great Staple Tor in afternoon light.

A great view from Sharpitor over Burrator. Dartmoor is fantastic for landscape photography as there are so many high natural viewpoints.

A quarry spill heap makes a great platform for photography. This view is towards Great Staple and Great Mis Tors.

Winter sun on the striking Logan Stones at Corndon Tor

During a long walk back to the car on a winter's evening I happened to glance left and caught the last light beyond a lone tree. The sky is often bathed with fantastic colour after the sun has actually set.

Sunset looking north towards Brentor Church which can just be seen in the distance.

I came across this gateway just after sunrise. Hound Tor sits in the shadows in the middle distance.

Looking towards
Chinkwell Tor
near Widecombe-
in-the-Moor.

A fine clear view to
Birch Tor over the
Warren House Inn.

A striking panorama looking over Great Staple Tor at sunset. Many Tors can be seen in the distance and on the horizon from here.

Widecombe-in-the-Moor on a grey Winters day. The road cannot be seen but the sign
lends a gentle warning of the steep hill down to the village.

Right:
Winter light can be the best of the year. I was fortunate to be around Scorhill early
on this particularly sunny morning as the sun broke over one of the standing stones.

A tremendous sky breaks over the Tor as the sun rises and illuminates the snow-dusted grass.

Thatched Church Cottage at Manaton, with St Winifreds Church behind.

Right:
A lone menhir (a prehistoric standing stone) in winter sunlight.

Merrivale and the quarry on a cold but sunny afternoon. Great Staple Tor towers behind.

Left:
The capital 'A' as I have named the big standing stone at the head of Merrivale stone rows. I had wanted to photograph the rows' in the snow and the sun for sometime before this perfect opportunity arose. These are the longest and most numerous rows on the moor.

Above:
Moretonhampstead Church of St Andrew
in the snow of February 2009.

Right:
Mist over Fernworthy as the sun gradually rises
over the water in early winter.

A scene that might be likened to a moonscape at Pil Tor. The fantastic cloud formations cradle the sun overhead.

Buried cars in Court Street, Moretonhampstead.

A strange phenomenon in the sky over Belstone.
An arch of light in the mist as the suns disappears behind thick, grey cloud.

A rich winter sunset looking over Haytor rocks.

Thick moss and fungi on branches. I have found moss over an inch thick on such branches.

Moss illuminated in the early light.

A plantation of old and new conifers.

A dramatic sunset casts an orange glow on the rocks.

I often come across old and disused agricultural vehicles around the moor. This one was found in a barn buried in tools and parts.

A well-preserved granite gateway near Bellever. Such gateposts had notches and holes into which wooden cross bars were fitted to keep in livestock.

This orange sunrise took my breath away. The light on the snow was extraordinary and the morning was completely still with not a whisper of wind.

Pathway through the
graveyard at Chagford.

People enjoying the snow
at Houndtor.

Ponies huddle together in the corner of a field surrounded by deep drifts.

Left:
View from Pil Tor. This is another favourite area as the landscape offers so many different angles and vistas from the tops of the many Tors.

Postbridge clapper bridge in the snow. This is the best known and most visited of all such bridges on Dartmoor.

The Powdermills near Postbridge. This is now a pottery and a gallery but many years ago it was the site of a gunpowder factory. The powder was used for blasting at the nearby granite quarries such as Foggintor, Swelltor and Merrivale. The isolated location away from inhabited areas is a clue to its previous use.

An open Dartmoor vista on cold and bright day.

Right:
One of my favourite images, taken from Leather Tor in early winter. The sun breaks
over the Tor and casts a wonderful light over the rocks and moss. Burrator lies
in the distance. Many days and hours spent on the moor occasionally
reward the photographer with that sought-after magical light.

Widecombe-in-the-Moor.

Slippery roads leading up on to the higher moorland. February 2009.

Left:
The North Teign on a very cold frosty morning. A faster shutter speed was used to capture the raging torrent. I was balanced on a very small rock and sharing it with a very large tripod.

A row of bare trees near Burrator. The low sun and soft winter light is ideal for capturing long shadows and contrast.

A bright day in November at Scorhill stone circle near Batworthy. One of the best preserved of the many prehistoric stone circles.

A steep walk to Sharp Tor was rewarded with a fantastic misty sunrise and great light on the rocks.

A superb vista from Sharpitor looking over towards Burrator reservoir.
The late afternoon light creates great contrast in the texture of the granite.

Sheep roam in the snow near the medieval settlement at Challacombe.

Sheep in the early morning frost near Princetown.

A wonderful light near Kings Tor as the sun sets on Boxing Day. Just as I set up the camera to take the shot of the distant Tors the sheep gathered in front of me. Luck sometimes plays a part.

A blizzard appears in seconds and catches me out in the open. I quickly took this and ran to the car.

I wandered through Chagford churchyard and gazed at the sheer volume of snow the had accumulated on the grave stones.

The early sun illuminates the frozen snow and tracks. Very slippery though…

110

Near Manaton, a tree is weighed down with thick snow.

Vista looking over towards Merrivale.

A snow-covered sign points the way at Hemsworthy Gate. Rippon Tor rises in the background.

Stones mark the remains of the Newhouse Inn. This meeting place was used by people travelling between Ashburton and Chagford. The inn burned to the ground around 1850.

A well-worn track in the snow leads towards the sun.

A few of the superb standing stones at Scorhill.
Watern Tor sits on the distant horizon.

The view from the top of Peek hill. Early winter colours paint the conifer forests below.

Bright sunlight pierces the rocks at Bellever Tor. The colours at sunset always seem to be more striking in winter. The sunstar phenomenon is created by the aperture blades in the camera lens.

Opposite:
A fantastic, dramatic sunset looking from Sheepstor. This tor is ideal for capturing sunsets as it is only a short walk back to the car. I have been so engrossed taking sunset shots elsewhere on the moor, then realising I am miles from the car in the dark.

Light on the rocks at Kes Tor. There is a very short space of time as the sun just breaks the horizon when you get a magical light for just a couple of minutes. You have to leave home very early and be there ready and waiting.

Opposite:
A low mist is lit up by the rising sun over Fernworthy reservoir.

Sunset in early Winter over the high moorland. The great height of the tors and their general accessibility makes them ideal platforms for great photography. Especially at either end of the day.

The Longstone on Chagford Common stands over 3 meters high. Kes Tor sits on the horizon.

Panorama looking up to Haytor rocks in mid February

Some of the nicest thatched cottages lie within North Bovey. An exceptionally attractive and unspoilt village set around a green and sitting on a hillside near the River Bovey.

Doccombe village centre in the snow of February 2009

The old telegraph office in Belstone which used to be the village Post Office.

A Land Rover passes through a cattle gate at Buckland. The sun creates a striking sky behind the trees.

Snow-draped trees on the road to the moor.

The River Walkham in early winter. This river isn't the easiest to reach but the valley through which it runs is beautiful. I regularly sank past my knees when I didn't look where I was walking.

Sunbeams break through a weathered tree. The trees constantly amaze me as to how and where they will grow. This one seemed to have sprung from the very centre of a huge granite boulder.

The green at Widecombe-in-the-Moor.

The Ten Commandments Stones on Buckland Beacon. One of the best and highest spots on the moor, it stands at 1253ft and was the site of a fire beacon. The ten commandments were carved into the dressed stones by the sculptor W.A. Clement in 1928. They are presently being redressed.

Above:
The famous Warren House Inn. The inn sits in a remote area 1425 ft above sea level and is thought to be the third highest in England. The original inn sat on the opposite side of the road and was rebuilt in its present position in 1845. I have had many a warm welcome here after a long walk over the moor.

Right:
The fireplace at the Warren House Inn which is said to have been burning continuously since 1845. This ancient watering hole is steeped in history and is blessed with a great atmosphere. They serve great ales too. Dartmoor has many amazing old public houses like this.

Sextons Cottage at Widecombe-in-the-Moor is now owned by the National Trust. The Church House was thought to have been built at the same time as the church tower in 1540. It has been a school house and alms houses.

Hound Tor is known as an 'avenue tor' as it comprises two separate rock masses. Its name was first recorded in Domesday book of 1086. The area around the tor is connected to a number of legends.

One of my all time favourites photographs that I feel is an iconic Dartmoor image. A bare lone tree silhouetted in the setting sun near Black Tor.

Sunset looking from Kings Tor across to Great Staple and Great Mis Tors. The long walk back to the car was a real joy.

Left:
A battered Land Rover sits in the snow on Ford Farm near Manaton. 'It still runs fine' the owner proudly told me.

Below:
Week Down Cross high above Chagford. It is not in its original location and once served as a wayside cross that marked a track from North Bovey and Moretonhampstead to Chagford.

Above:
The remains of the engine house at Wheal Betsy Tin mine beside the Tavistock road. This is known as the leaning tower of Dartmoor due to the characteristic tilt of the chimney. It was the engine house for the mine that operated from 1740 until 1877 on the site. It produced over 53 000 ounces of silver and 4000 tons of pig lead.

Right:
I got caught in an extremely heavy blizzard as I photographed Bennetts Cross. It was a complete white out as I walked back to the car. I almost fell into a large snow-filled ditch.

Left:
The sign post that greets you on the green as you arrive at Widecombe-in-the-Moor.

Below:
Looking over Merrivale with the first light snow of Winter

Above:
Trees picked out by the snow in a scene resembling a winter wonderland.

Left:
A lone figure stands on Haytor in the last snow of Winter

Rushing water and winter colours at Buckland bridge.

Snow sits amongst the yellow flowers of the winter gorse.

View from Staple Tor late in the afternoon.

Howell Tor under a full moon with Haytor in the distance.

Howell Tor is a short walk beyond Saddle Tor.

Wonderful patterns created by the drifting snow on the gorse hidden beneath.